WINE
FLIES
WHEN YOU'RE HAVING
FUN

RECIPES • PROJECTS • FUN FACTS

Luckily for wine lovers, grapevines flourish in many parts of the world. That includes places like Europe, Asia, South Africa, Australia, New Zealand, the Balkans, the Mediterranean, and large portions of North and South America. The cooler climates typically produce tart, more acidic wines, whereas grapes grown in warmer climates produce wines with a more in-your-face fruit flavor.

What's that mean for you? A huge variety of wines to choose from. Try a few from different regions to see what you prefer.

The fun is in the tasting!

Printed in the United States of America
by G&R Publishing Co.

Distributed By:

507 Industrial Street
Waverly, IA 50677

ISBN-13: 978-1-56383-550-6
Item #3699

When wine flies...

You like drinking wine. But let's face it, there will come a time when you look in the fridge and realize there has been an open bottle of your favorite hiding behind the milk *(gasp)*! What do you do with that last little bit? Don't throw it out!

Use that wine to make oodles of delicious snacks, appetizers, desserts, and drinks to share with your friends. And the bonus? Pour a glass from a fresh bottle of the same wine and you'll enjoy a perfectly created food-wine pairing!

Then save your corks and empty bottles so you can do fun things with them – both decorative and practical. But beware – you might find yourself drinking more wine just for those bottles and corks!

So enjoy a good glass of wine anytime *(and consider slipping a bottle behind the milk once in a while)*.

there's fun in the air!

Party Pizza with Cracker Crust

1 lb. boneless chicken breast, diced

1 C. red wine, divided

1 (6 oz.) can tomato paste

Black pepper

1 (14.5 oz.) can crushed Italian-style tomatoes

1 (9 oz.) box Triscuit crackers

Your favorite pizza toppings *(we used black olives, mushrooms & green onions)*

Your favorite shredded cheese

Grated Parmesan cheese

To Make

Cook the chicken in ¼ cup wine over medium heat until done. In the meantime, in a saucepan, whisk together the tomato paste, the remaining ¾ cup wine, and a few shakes of pepper. Stir in the tomatoes and bring to a boil over high heat. Reduce heat and simmer for 10 minutes, stirring occasionally.

Preheat the oven to 350° and line a 10 x 15" rimmed baking sheet with foil. Line up the Triscuits side by side on the prepped baking sheet until it's pretty much covered. Drizzle as much of the hot tomato sauce as you'd like over the crackers, just like you would with a regular pizza *(but this is no regular pizza, folks)*. Add the cooked chicken, toppings, and cheeses.

Bake for 10 to 15 minutes or until everything is hot and the cheese is melted to your liking. Enjoy these hot from the oven. Be civilized and use a spatula or just grab 'em off the pan. Either way, it's all good!

We used Sangiovese for this recipe. You could also try Lambrusco.

CRACKED WINE COOKIES

½ C. vegetable shortening

1⅔ C. sugar

2 tsp. vanilla

2 eggs

2 oz. unsweetened baking chocolate, melted

2 C. flour

2 tsp. baking powder

½ tsp. plus ⅛ tsp. salt

⅓ C. red wine

Powdered sugar

To Make

Beat the shortening, sugar, and vanilla until light and fluffy. Add the eggs and chocolate, beating constantly.

In a separate bowl, stir together the flour, baking powder, and salt. Add to the creamed mixture alternately with the wine until well combined. Cover and chill about 3 hours.

Preheat the oven to 350°. Grease two cookie sheets and pour some powdered sugar into a bowl.

Roll chilled dough into 1¼" balls and spin 'em around in the powdered sugar to coat heavily. Arrange them on the prepped cookie sheets. Bake for 11 to 14 minutes or until they're cracked on top. Let them set on the cookie sheets for 5 minutes, then move to a rack to cool.

Let cookie sheets cool between batches or the dough will melt before it hits the oven. While we love melty chocolate, cookies will look flat and sad if they start off as a messy blob.

These cookies were delicious tested with Tawny Port, but feel free to experiment with other Ports or other reds altogether.

DID YOU KNOW?

Tawny Port has been
aged at least 10 years.
It's mellow and nutty with
slight woody and dried
fruit characteristics.

Corky Coasters

Corks

Locking pliers, optional

Sharp knife

*Flat cork can be purchased in sheet or roll form.

Flat cork*

Hot glue gun and glue

X-Acto knife

Want to make a trivet? Just keep adding cut corks until it's the size you'd like.

To Make

1. Choose your corks.

   Your best bet: For each coaster, choose four corks that are the same length and circumference. Don't use corks that are tapered at one end.

2. Cut the corks in half lengthwise *(get those halves as even as possible)*.

   Make it safe: Lock a cork into the pliers so it's nice and tight, then hold on. Cut through the middle of the cork using the sharp knife.

3. Lay the corks cut side down on the flat cork in a pattern you like. Hot glue in place.

   Note: Hot glue bonds the cut side of corks well, so it's a good fit for this project.

4. Use the X-Acto knife to cut straight lines around the outside of the corks, through the flat cork, to create a nice square coaster.

5. Make more!

Be sure to cut on a cutting board to protect your work surface.

9

Spanish Strawberry Sangria

Chill a bottle of lemon-flavored carbonated water. In a pitcher or punch bowl, mix 2 (750 mL) bottles fruity red wine *(we used Spanish Rioja)*, ¾ cup brandy, and ½ cup orange liqueur. Juice one orange and slice another one; add to the pitcher along with a sliced lemon and 1 pound sliced strawberries. Cover and chill for several hours. To serve, stir and pour into ice-filled glasses. Add some fruit and a little of the chilled carbonated water to each glass.

Sparkling Watermelon Sangria

Chill a (750 mL) bottle of sparkling wine *(we used Moscato d'Asti)*. Cut a seedless watermelon into chunks and place into a big pitcher or punch bowl. Pour in 3 (750 mL) bottles of a fruity rosé wine; cover and chill for several hours. To serve, stir 1½ cups of the chilled sparkling wine into the pitcher. Pour into ice-filled glasses and add some watermelon chunks.

Poor Man's Sangria: Mix equal parts Coke and red wine *(we used Malbec)*. Serve over ice with a splash of lemon juice and a cherry. Instant single-serving refreshment!

Cheesy Garlic Bites

2 (7.5 oz.) tubes refrigerated buttermilk biscuits

Pepper Jack or mozzarella cheese, cut into ¾" cubes

3 T. olive oil

1 T. minced garlic

Red pepper flakes to taste

2 T. butter

¼ C. white wine

Salt

½ C. grated Parmesan cheese

1 C. shredded mozzarella cheese

Chopped fresh basil to taste

To Make

Preheat the oven to 450°. Flatten each biscuit slightly and put a cheese cube in the center. Wrap the dough around the cheese to form a ball and pinch the edges to seal in that cheese.

Heat the oil in a skillet over medium-low heat. Add the garlic and a pinch or two of pepper flakes; sauté for a couple of minutes. Add the butter and stir until it melts. Pour in the wine and add ¼ teaspoon salt. Heat for another minute or two, then turn off the heat.

Roll each dough ball in the buttery wine mixture and set into a mini muffin cup, pinched side up. Set the remaining butter mixture aside – you'll want it later. Stir together the Parmesan and shredded mozzarella and mound some onto each biscuit. Bake for 10 to 15 minutes or until golden brown.

Pull them out of the oven and brush them with that delicious butter mixture in the skillet. Use it all up – there's a lot of flavor in there. Now sprinkle with a little salt and basil. Enjoy hot.

This recipe was tested using Riesling. Any other light and fruity white would work well, too.

Fruit Slush with Chocolate Cream

1 C. red wine, chilled
1½ C. frozen raspberries
1 C. crushed ice

Powdered sugar
½ C. heavy cream
1 T. chocolate syrup, chilled

To Make

In a blender, combine the wine and raspberries until relatively smooth. *(If those raspberry seeds bother you, you can push the mixture through a mesh strainer to remove most of them.)*

Add the ice to the slush in the blender and blend until smooth. Taste. Blend in 2 to 3 teaspoons powdered sugar if you want it sweeter. Pop the whole thing into the freezer.

In a chilled bowl using chilled beaters, whip the cream, chocolate syrup, and 2 teaspoons powdered sugar until soft peaks form.

Pour slush into glasses and top with chocolate cream.

Need to chill a bottle fast?

Wrap a wet paper towel around a bottle of wine and set it in the freezer. This method can chill a room-temperature bottle as much as 15° in 15 minutes!

14

We used a sweet Rosso for this recipe.

DID YOU KNOW?

Combining chocolate
syrup and whipping cream
makes a yummy topping,
and it whips up beautifully.
Our cream has a mild
chocolate-y flavor. Whip in
more chocolate syrup if you
want more intense flavor.

planter on page 42

Signature Cork Letter

Cardboard letter
  *(ours was 6½" wide x 8" tall
  x ⁵/₁₆" thick)*

Brown craft (or latex) paint

Foam brush

Photo hangers, optional

Variety of corks

Sharp and serrated knives

Wood glue *(we used Elmer's
  Craft Bond)*

Clear acrylic spray

16

To Make

1. Give your cardboard letter a thin coat of paint with the brush and let it dry.

2. If you want to hang this letter on a wall, attach hangers to the back side now.

3. Gather interesting corks and cork pieces and arrange them as you'd like to cover the letter.

   Make it fun: Mix them up and turn some sideways. Break a few corks and/or use the sharp knife to slice them into smaller chunks and thin disks that will fit together and fill in small spaces. Cut out words, images, or numbers that have special meaning to you.

4. When you like your design, glue the corks in place using a generous amount of glue. Let dry completely, at least 6 hours.

5. With the serrated knife, carefully trim off any corks that extend past the edge of the letter so edges are even.

6. For a smooth finish, coat with acrylic spray following directions on the can.

This glue dries clear. Make sure yours does, too.

17

MAKES 25

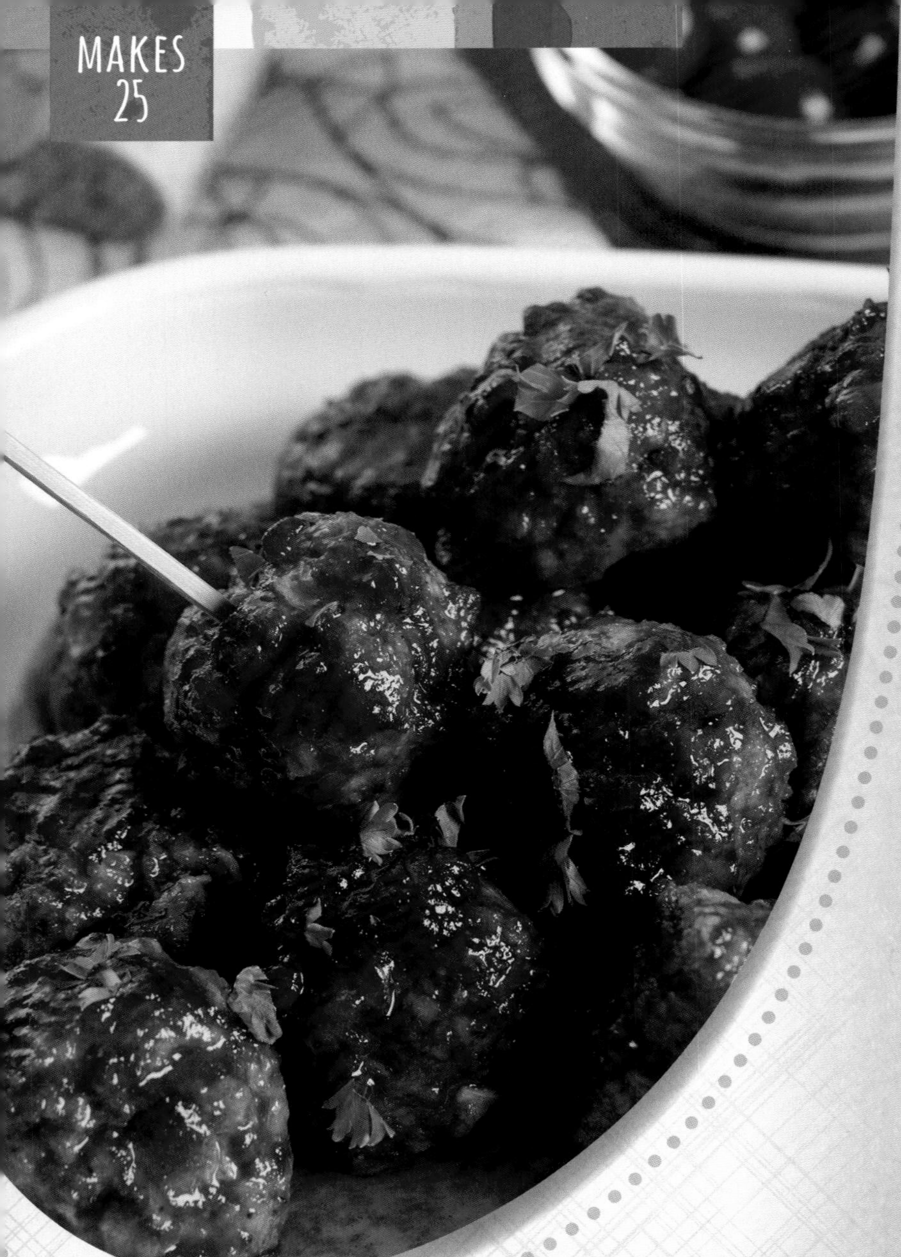

Cranberry Party Meatballs

1 lb. extra lean ground beef
¾ C. soft bread crumbs
¼ C. finely chopped celery
¼ C. finely chopped onion
1 egg
1½ tsp. Worcestershire sauce

1 tsp. garlic salt
½ tsp. black pepper
Red wine
½ (14 oz.) can whole cranberry sauce
½ C. brown sugar
1 tsp. hot Chinese mustard

To Make

Preheat the oven to 375°. Lightly grease a large shallow baking pan.

In a big bowl, combine ground beef, bread crumbs, celery, onion, egg, Worcestershire sauce, garlic salt, pepper, and a splash or two of wine. Mix with your hands until just blended. Shape into 1" balls and arrange on the prepped pan.

Bake for 20 minutes or until done. Have a glass of wine while you stir together the cranberry sauce, brown sugar, mustard, and ½ cup wine in a saucepan. Simmer for 5 minutes, stirring often.

Put the meatballs into a slow cooker and pour the wine sauce over the top. Keep warm over low heat during serving.

We tested these using Pinot Noir. Have a different red in the house? Give it a try.

19

Mini Wine Loaves

3 C. sifted bread flour

1 T. baking powder

2 T. sugar

1 tsp. salt

1⅓ C. plus 1 T. white wine, divided

2 to 3 tsp. melted butter

4 oz. cream cheese, softened

Fresh pear slices

Honey

Chopped hazelnuts (a.k.a. filberts)

To Make

Preheat the oven to 375°. Grease and flour two (3 x 5") mini loaf pans.

Whisk together the flour, baking powder, sugar, and salt. Stir in 1⅓ cups wine (pour yourself a glass, too).

Divide the dough in half and put each half into a prepped loaf pan; brush with the butter and pop those little guys into the oven. Bake for 40 minutes, until they test done with a toothpick and the tops are toasty. Let cool 5 minutes before removing the bread from the pans. Cool completely, then slice.

Beat together the cream cheese and the remaining 1 tablespoon wine. Spread evenly over the bread slices and top each with a pear slice. Drizzle with a little honey, and toss on a few hazelnuts.

We used a full-bodied white Viognier for this recipe. Chardonnay would be another good choice.

perfectly suited
for fun toppings

TRY RED WINE

You can make these loaves
with your favorite red
wine, too; keep in mind
that your bread will be a
purple-ish color, but it will
still taste great.

21

POUR-SPOUT DISPENSER

Wash out an empty wine bottle and remove the label and glue residue *(see page 63 for easy instructions)*. Etch a design or words on the bottle following the directions for your particular etching cream. Fill your bottle as desired *(ours is filled with olive oil)* and push a liquor pourer *(not the measured kind)* into the top. It's convenient and pretty enough to keep on your countertop all the time.

Hardware Key Chain

Drill a ¼" hole lengthwise through an interesting wine or champagne cork. Insert a ¼ x 3" eye screw until it comes out the other end and the eye is snug against the cork. Attach a washer on the end of the screw, and follow up with a ¼" nut; screw it on tight. Attach your keys and hit the road!

For extra hold, try running a bead of glue around the screw before attaching the nut.

23

cheesecake inside makes these super yummy

Remember that the freezing process doesn't affect the alcohol content, so make sure the kiddos don't get their hands on these. The adults, however, will enjoy them immensely!

Blueberry Cheesecake Winesicles

2 C. fresh blueberries

½ C. red wine

¼ C. simple syrup

¼ C. heavy cream

4 tsp. sugar

2½ oz. cream cheese, softened

¼ C. graham cracker crumbs

To Make

In a blender, combine blueberries, wine, and simple syrup. Puree until relatively smooth; set aside.

In a chilled bowl using chilled beaters, beat together the cream and sugar until soft peaks form. In a separate bowl, beat the cream cheese until light and fluffy. Fold the cream cheese into the whipped cream. Measure ¼ cup of this mixture into a small bowl and stir in the cracker crumbs.

Pour a little wine mixture into each popsicle mold. Then add a little cream cheese mixture and a little cracker mixture. Keep layering until the molds are nearly full. Cover and push popsicle sticks down the middle. Pop 'em in the freezer overnight.

Remove the pops from the molds and enjoy.

To make simple syrup

Heat equal parts water and sugar over medium heat until the sugar dissolves. Cool before using. You can keep any extra tightly covered in the fridge for a couple of weeks.

25

Pork-Stuffed Mushrooms

24 oz. whole button or baby Portobello mushrooms

¾ lb. ground pork sausage

½ onion, finely diced

2 tsp. minced garlic

⅔ C. white wine

Salt & black pepper to taste

1 (8 oz.) pkg. cream cheese, softened

1 egg yolk

¾ C. grated Parmesan cheese, plain or seasoned

To Make

Remove and chop the mushroom stems. Set the caps on a greased baking sheet. Set all aside.

In a medium skillet, brown the sausage, breaking it apart while it cooks; remove from the skillet and set aside to cool. In the same skillet, cook the onion and garlic for 2 minutes over medium-low heat. Add the wine and cook 5 minutes longer or until the liquid has evaporated. Add the chopped mushroom stems and cook for 2 minutes. Season with salt and pepper. Set aside to cool.

In a bowl, stir together the cream cheese, egg yolk, and Parmesan cheese. Stir in the cooled sausage and the mushroom mixture. Refrigerate until cold.

Preheat the oven to 350°. Mound the sausage mixture into the mushroom caps and bake for 20 to 25 minutes or until golden brown. Serve hot with a glass of white wine.

We tested this recipe using a Sauvignon Blanc. What's your favorite dry white? Give it a try!

DID YOU KNOW?

Using a dry white wine for cooking assures you're not adding sweetness to a savory dish. Anytime you cook using wine you love, you know a glass of that same wine is going to taste amazing paired with your meal.

DID YOU KNOW?

Wine not only adds
flavor to fondue, but
because of its acidity, it
keeps the cheese from
curdling and getting
stringy. Knowing all of
that, will you ever make
fondue without wine?
We didn't think so.

Spirited 2-Cheese Fondue

⅓ C. fruit brandy or dry white vermouth

¼ C. cornstarch

White pepper

2 C. white wine

1 small garlic clove, minced

½ lb. Swiss cheese, shredded

½ lb. Gruyère cheese, shredded

Dippers*

To Make

Pour the brandy or vermouth into a small bowl and stir in the cornstarch and a few pinches of white pepper until dissolved; set aside.

Heat the wine and garlic in a saucepan over medium heat until just barely simmering *(don't let it boil)*. Add both cheeses, a handful at a time, stirring until melted before adding more. When all the cheese has melted, stir the cornstarch mixture again and slowly add it to the cheesy wine, stirring constantly until thickened and silky, about 5 minutes.

Transfer to a fondue pot, light that burner, and start dipping.

* Use French bread, pineapple, apples & pears if using brandy; sourdough bread, broccoli & peppers if using vermouth.

> *To infuse white wine, remove ½ cup wine from a bottle. Add ⅓ cup sugar, 8 coriander seeds, and the zest of an orange. Recork. Swirl to dissolve sugar and chill for a week, swirling once a day. Strain before drinking.*

Sauvignon Blanc was the wine of choice for testing fondue and infused wine.

Cherry Red Float

Chill a 750 mL bottle of sparkling red wine *(we used a fruity Rosa Regale)*.

For each float, muddle a few maraschino cherries in the bottom of a glass. Add a few scoops of vanilla ice cream and a few more cherries; top it off with some of the chilled wine.

Top with whipped cream and a cherry, just because it's delicious and pretty. Now kick back and enjoy.

Fruit Salsa & Cinnamon Crisps

Preheat the oven to 400°. Cut four (7") flour tortillas into eight wedges each; arrange them on baking sheets, coat with cooking spray, and sprinkle with cinnamon-sugar. Bake for 8 minutes or until crisp; cool.

Peel and dice 1 Granny Smith apple, 2 kiwi, and 1 mango; place them in a bowl with 1½ cups diced strawberries. Sprinkle with 1 tablespoon brown sugar and ¼ teaspoon cinnamon; toss to coat. Stir in ¼ cup fruity red wine *(try Zinfandel)* and chill. Serve with the cooled cinnamon crisps. De-lish-ous!

31

use pendants from page 48

safety pins keep it snug

How to Wrap a Wine Bottle

Lay a tea towel on a flat surface, wrong side up; fold up the bottom edge so the towel is about 3" taller than the bottle. Lay the bottle at the left edge of the towel, placing the bottom of the bottle even with the fold. Roll the towel tightly around the bottle, stopping a few inches from the end. Fold that end over toward the bottle so you have a nice finished edge. Roll the bottle to the edge and secure with safety pins. Tie a rope or ribbon around the top and add a couple of wine glass charms to complete the theme.

How to Clink

Anatomy 101

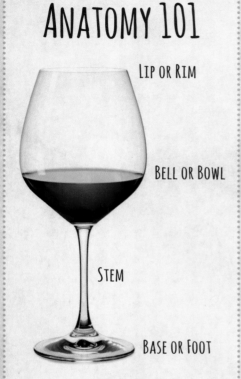

- Lip or Rim
- Bell or Bowl
- Stem
- Base or Foot

"Lips" are for drinking

"Bells" are for clinking

Does correct clinking really matter? Yup!

1) That lip is fragile. A wrong clink and you could end up with a wine-glass-clinking disaster.

2) A clink at the wrong angle could lead to spilling that wonderful, precious wine.

3) But, a clink at the bell sounds like a bell, and it marks the start of a very satisfying experience.

So, find a clinking partner. Practice makes perfect!

GENERAL TASTING GUIDE

WINE CATEGORIES

SPARKLING   **DRY WHITE**   **SWEET WHITE**   **RICH WHITE**

FOOD & WINE PAIRING

SERVING TEMPERATURE

  F°

 43–47°F 43–52°F

Keep in mind that wine pairings are ultimately your personal preference. So if you don't like a suggested pairing, by all means, switch to something else. They're your taste buds and you need to keep them happy, no matter what anybody else says.

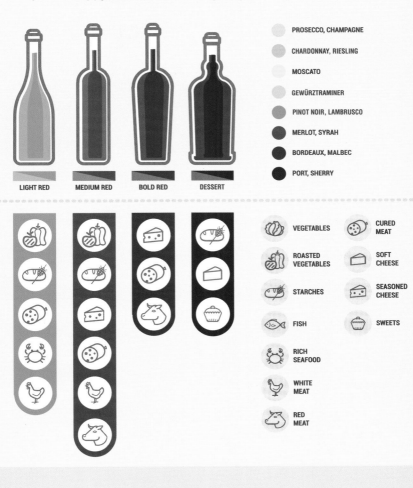

PROSECCO, CHAMPAGNE

CHARDONNAY, RIESLING

MOSCATO

GEWÜRZTRAMINER

PINOT NOIR, LAMBRUSCO

MERLOT, SYRAH

BORDEAUX, MALBEC

PORT, SHERRY

LIGHT RED   MEDIUM RED   BOLD RED   DESSERT

VEGETABLES   CURED MEAT

ROASTED VEGETABLES SOFT CHEESE

STARCHES   SEASONED CHEESE

FISH   SWEETS

RICH SEAFOOD

WHITE MEAT

RED MEAT

54–61°F   63–65°F   50–65°F

What kind of wine drinker are you?
Take this fun quiz to find out.

1) HOW DO YOU USUALLY DRINK WINE?

   a. If it's warm, I throw in an ice cube. Bring it on!
   b. I usually chill everything, but can drink room temperature wine if I have to.
   c. Room temperature for my reds. For the rest, I have lovely ice buckets.
   d. The correct temperature matters.

2) WHERE DO YOU DRINK WINE?

   a. Anywhere. Anytime.
   b. Wherever there are lots of people.
   c. With a few friends, around a cozy fire.
   d. Friends and colleagues come to my home bar.

3) WHERE IS YOUR WINE STORED?

   a. Am I supposed to store wine? I drink it as soon as I buy it!
   b. A few in the fridge; a few in the cupboard.
   c. Not enough room for everything, so they're still in their boxes.
   d. In a climate-controlled wine cellar.

4) WHAT TYPE OF WINE DO YOU DRINK?

   a. Right now? I'm not sure, but it's delicious!
   b. White is my delight, but I'm into trying new things.
   c. Red. Absolutely.
   d. I have a nice collection of rare wines, everything aged to perfection.

5) WHAT ARE YOUR WINE GLASSES LIKE?

   a. Um, I think I'm using juice glasses.
   b. A set for red; a set for white.
   c. Very pretty. Very classy.
   d. I have something for every varietal.

6 HOW DO YOU SERVE WINE?

a. Open. Pour. Drink.
b. I let the bottle set a few minutes between opening and serving.
c. I have beautiful decanters, so I use them.
d. Decanting wines properly brings out their best qualities.

7 WHERE DO YOU BUY YOUR WINE?

a. Anywhere convenient, like the convenience store down the street.
b. You can buy very nice wines at a reasonable price any number of places.
c. I like the local liquor store; the owner knows me and treats me right.
d. Mostly on trips to Italy.

Moment of truth: if your answers were...

MOSTLY A'S

You're the life of the party. You might have a tendency to chug your wine. But if you're happy, that's what really matters.

MOSTLY B'S

You're open-minded and adaptable. You'll try just about anything once and will never ever turn down a glass of wine.

MOSTLY C'S

You're a wine lover who probably outgrew the taste of sweet wine years ago. You like nice things and might just have an artsy side.

MOSTLY D'S

You're a serious wine hipster (some might call you a wine snob or cork dork, but we won't judge you).

A MIX

You might be a bit eclectic and feel that diversity makes the world go 'round. Why be tied to one style when you can have it all?

Hot Red Cocoa

In a saucepan over low heat, combine 6 ounces finely
chopped bittersweet chocolate baking bar and ⅓ cup fruity
red wine *(we tried it with Pinot Noir)*; whisk until melted and
smooth. Stir in 1 cup milk, a pinch of salt, and ⅔ cup water.
Bring to a low boil and whisk for 3 minutes. Stir in 3 to 4
teaspoons sugar and ¼ cup orange juice, heating until it
reaches your desired serving temperature and the sugar is
dissolved.

Try it frozen! Mix as directed, cool, pour into a lidded
container, and freeze.

To serve in orange halves, cut 5 oranges across the middle, scoop out the insides, and pop the shells into the freezer until they're well chilled. Then fill with orange ice.

Orange Ice

In a 9 x 13" pan, whisk together 1 (750 mL) bottle white wine *(we used Sauvignon Blanc)*, 3 tablespoons frozen orange juice concentrate, 1 tablespoon frozen limeade concentrate, 1 cup peach nectar, 1 teaspoon clear vanilla, and 3 tablespoons honey. Cover and freeze about 4 hours or until scoopable, stirring with a fork every hour.

Mushroom Bites

1 leek

¼ lb. Brie cheese

1 (15 ct.) pkg. mini phyllo shells

2 T. butter

1 tsp. minced garlic

8 oz. of your favorite mushrooms, chopped

Salt & black pepper to taste

½ C. red wine

2 tsp. chopped fresh chives or thyme

To Make

Preheat the oven to 350°. While you wait, finely dice the white part of the leek and rinse under cool running water. Remove the rind from the cheese *(the rind is edible, but it won't melt)* and cut the Brie into small pieces. Arrange the shells on a small baking sheet and bake for 5 minutes. Set all aside.

Melt the butter in a small skillet over medium heat. Add the set-aside leek and cook on medium heat for 5 minutes or until tender. Add the garlic, mushrooms, salt, and pepper; cook for 5 minutes. Increase the heat to medium-high, add the wine and chives, and cook 15 minutes longer, until most of the liquid has evaporated. Divide the mixture evenly among the shells. Top each with pieces of the set-aside Brie. Bake 5 to 8 minutes, until the cheese has melted. Serve hot.

Freeze wine in ice cube trays and store the cubes in a resealable plastic freezer bag to use in recipes like this. Each compartment in a standard tray holds about 1 oz. (2 T.) of liquid. Substitute four cubes for the wine in this recipe.

This recipe was tested with Merlot, but feel free to try it with any medium-bodied dry red.

TRY THIS

Instead of baking the filling in shells, just cook the mushrooms in the wine as directed, then toss the cut-up Brie into the skillet until melted. Scoop it up with hefty crackers.

Wine-Loving Planters

Use a pretty wine glass to pot up your favorite succulent in sandy soil, or attach an air plant to a favorite cork using glue *(for best results use a florist-type pan glue)*. Set your plants in a sunny location and water or mist as needed.

Cork or Screw Cap?

The method used to cap a bottle of wine isn't an indication of the wine's quality. That's good news! Now you can pop or twist without any doubts.

Corked Magnets

To make a handy pencil holder for your fridge or file cabinet, use a drill to hollow out the center of a cork *(½" is best, but ⅜" will work in a pinch)*, but don't drill all the way through. Attach a flexible adhesive magnet to the back and tuck a short pencil into the hole. No drill? No problem. You can just put a magnet on the back of a whole or halved cork, too. These quirky corks will remind you of all the delicious wine you've enjoyed.

MAKES 15

try powdered sugar
or ground nuts

DID YOU KNOW?

Legend tells us that the
chocolate truffle was an
accidental *(but, oh-so
wonderful)* French creation,
named for its resemblance
to the luxurious black edible
fungus called a truffle. While
these truffles are luxurious,
they taste nothing like their
supposed namesake! Thank
you chocolate and wine!

Chocoholic Truffles

4 oz. bittersweet or semi-sweet baking chocolate, coarsely chopped

2½ T. heavy cream

2½ T. dry red wine

1 tsp. powdered sugar

¼ tsp. vanilla

⅛ tsp. espresso powder

Unsweetened cocoa powder

To Make

Place the chopped chocolate in a small mixing bowl. Heat the cream in the microwave until just boiling and pour over the chocolate. Let that set for a minute or two to soften a bit, then microwave in 15-second intervals until nearly melted. Whisk to melt completely. Stir in the wine, powdered sugar, vanilla, and espresso powder until smooth. Cover and chill for an hour or two.

Line a tray with parchment paper and pour some cocoa powder into a bowl. Roll the chilled mixture into 1" balls, coat with cocoa powder, and arrange on the prepped tray. Chill for at least 30 minutes, then coat again with cocoa powder.

That wine you used to make the truffles? Pour yourself a glass to drink along with them. You won't believe how one impacts the other. Guaranteed amazing!

We tried this recipe using Malbec. Syrah or any other full-bodied, dark fruited red would work, too.

Texas Caviar

Drain and rinse 2 (15 oz.) cans each black eyed peas and whole kernel corn and 1 (15 oz.) can black beans. Dice 1 each red onion, green and red bell pepper, and jalapeño pepper. Toss everything together in a big bowl. Add 2½ teaspoons minced garlic and ¼ cup chopped cilantro. Pour ⅓ cup white wine *(try a buttery Chardonnay)* into a small bowl; drizzle in 1 tablespoon olive oil while whisking vigorously. Stir in 2 teaspoons coarse salt, 1 teaspoon black pepper, and the juice of 1 lime; mix into the veggies and chill. Serve with tortilla chips.

Port Wine Cheese Ball

Place 1 cup finely chopped walnuts or pecans in a dry skillet.
Heat over medium heat 8 to 10 minutes, tossing until nuts are
lightly toasted; let cool.

Put 1 cup shredded sharp cheddar cheese, 4 ounces cream
cheese, 2½ tablespoons Port wine *(we used Tawny Port)*, and
1½ teaspoons Worcestershire sauce in a food processor. Process
1 minute, scraping the bowl as needed. Chill several hours.
Roll the cheese into a ball and coat with the cooled
nuts. Wrap with plastic wrap and chill 2 hours longer.
*(To serve as a spread instead, press the cheese
mixture into a shallow bowl, with or without nuts.)*

you can decorate both sides if you'd like

SIPPER'S PENDANTS

Corks

Sharp knife

Large binder clip, optional

Sandpaper, optional

Rubber stamp & ink pad

Acrylic paint

Foam brush

1 tiny eye screw for each pendant

1 necklace chain for each pendant

Check this out! Some corks have a design pre-stamped on the end! Just slice and add hardware!

To Make

(1) Cut cork into slices about ³⁄₈" thick.

Make it easy: Clamp the binder clip over the length of the cork, making sure both are flush against a cutting board. With one end of the cork extending beyond the clip about ³⁄₈", use a sawing motion to cut the cork with the knife. The straight edge of the clip will give you a nice straight guide for cutting. As you get close to the end of the cork, put another cork behind it to prevent the clip from snapping off.

(2) Use sandpaper to smooth out the cut side of the cork, if needed.

(3) Decorate the flat side of each cork.

Make it pretty: Use a stamp and ink pad *(we used an acid-free pigment ink)* to stamp designs directly onto the cork, or paint it first.

(4) When dry, turn an eye screw into the top of the pendant and slip a necklace chain through it.

anything goes... be creative when decorating.

Sweet & Sassy Merlot Mix

- 2⅔ C. Rice Chex cereal
- 2⅔ C. nuts (*we used almonds, pecans & cashews*)
- 2 T. unsalted butter
- ⅓ C. dark brown sugar
- ⅓ C. plus 1 T. red wine
- 2 T. pure maple syrup
- 1 T. unsweetened cocoa powder
- 1 tsp. ground allspice
- ¼ tsp. each ground cayenne pepper, ginger, cloves & cinnamon
- 2⅔ C. pretzels
- 1⅓ C. oyster crackers
- 1 tsp. coarse salt

To Make

Preheat the oven to 350° and line a couple of rimmed baking sheets with parchment paper; put them to the side. Put the Rice Chex and nuts in a big bowl and set those aside as well.

Melt the butter in a saucepan over medium heat. Add the brown sugar and wine. Bring to a simmer and heat for 3 minutes, stirring occasionally. Remove the saucepan from the heat and whisk in the maple syrup, cocoa powder, allspice, cayenne, ginger, cloves, and cinnamon. Pour this over the mixture in the bowl, stirring to coat. Add the pretzels and crackers to the bowl and stir it all together until coated, sprinkling in the salt as you stir.

Divide among the prepped baking sheets, spreading out in a single layer. Bake for 15 minutes, stirring twice. Turn the oven off and open the door. Leave the pans in the oven for another 5 minutes, and then take them out to cool.

As shown in the title, we used Merlot in this recipe.

MERLOMENT [MER-LOH-MENT]

That moment in time when your judgment
may have been affected by drinking too
much wine.

51

Saucy Ginger Wings

Preheat the oven to 400°. Arrange 3 pounds thawed chicken wing pieces skin side down on a foil-lined, greased rimmed baking sheet.

In a small saucepan over medium-low heat, mix ⅔ cup soy sauce, ½ cup dry red wine *(we used Sangiovese)*, ¼ cup plus 1½ teaspoons sugar, and ⅛ teaspoon ground ginger, stirring until hot; pour evenly over the wings. Bake for 45 minutes; flip and bake 45 minutes longer, until the sauce is thick and sticky.

Brain Freeze Riesling Cream

Whisk together ¾ cup white wine *(Riesling)* and 3 heaping tablespoons superfine sugar in a big bowl until the sugar dissolves. Gradually whisk in 1¼ cups heavy cream until it begins to thicken. Transfer to a container with a lid and freeze several hours, until hard.

Scoop into bowls and add fresh berries and a splash of wine, if you'd like.

No ice cream machine needed.

Odd-sized spaces? Cut ends from corks to fit just right.

GET HOOKED CORK BOARD

Frame of your choice

Foam core board or thin plywood, optional

Photo hangers, optional

Wood glue or tacky glue *(we used Elmer's Craft Bond wood glue)*

Drill

Cup hooks

Corks

Could be used as a tray, too! Just leave off the hangers & hooks.

54

To Make

1. If your frame has a wooden backing board and a hanger, you're in luck! If not, cut a piece of foam board or plywood to fit the frame. Attach it to the back of the frame with wood glue; let dry. Then mount a hanger on the back of the frame, if needed.

2. Drill pilot holes in the bottom of the frame and screw in cup hooks.

3. Mess around with your cast-off corks, fitting them inside the frame's opening against the foam board. Trim corks to fit, if necessary. *(See page 49 to make it easy.)*

   Important: Make sure you don't cut off important words or pictures when you trim the corks – you'll want all of those to show when your board is complete.

4. Once you have an arrangement you like, lift one or two corks at a time, add glue, and put them back in place with important words or pictures facing out.

   Make it easy: Lift corks from the center by poking a push pin into them and lifting.

   Continue until all the corks are glued in place. Let the glue dry several hours before hanging.

DID YOU KNOW?

You can tell the doneness of shrimp not only by its pink color, but also by its shape. If it looks like a "U," it's Undercooked; an "O" means it's Overcooked; and a "C" means it's Correct.

Shrimp & Drunken Grapes

12 green seedless grapes

1 (750 mL) bottle white wine

1 tsp. each dried rosemary,
thyme, oregano, basil,
marjoram & fennel seed

1 C. water

12 large raw shrimp,
peeled & deveined,
thawed if frozen

To Make

Put the grapes into a bowl and add enough wine to just cover them. Chill at least 2 hours.

Put the rosemary, thyme, oregano, basil, marjoram, and fennel seed into a spice or coffee grinder; grind until powdery. Toss the spice blend into a medium saucepan. Add the water and 2 cups of wine. Bring to a boil, then turn down the heat to a simmer. Add the shrimp and heat for just a few minutes until they are pink and cooked; drain and chill.

To assemble, tuck a grape into the curl of each shrimp and attach with a pick. Serve chilled or at room temperature.

Need to chill a glass of wine quickly?

Adding a few frozen grapes to a glass of room-temperature wine will chill it nearly 30° in just 2 minutes! Bonus: no ice cubes to water down your wine.

This recipe was tested using a bottle of Pinot Grigio, but any medium-bodied dry white would work.

CRAN-APPLE SANGRIA

In a pitcher or punch bowl, stir together 2 (750 mL) bottles white wine *(we used Grüner Veltliner)* and 1 (750 mL) bottle sparkling cider. Add 1 sliced and seeded orange, 1 cup fresh or frozen cranberries, and several mint leaves. Cover and chill several hours before serving. Ahhhhh…

I Bottle of Wine
= *2.4 lbs. of grapes*
= *4 glasses of wine*
= *a couple of happy people*

Fuzzy Navel Sangria

In a pitcher or punch bowl, stir together 1 (750 mL) bottle dry white wine *(recipe tested with Pinot Grigio)*, ¾ cup peach schnapps, ¼ cup brandy, and 1 cup orange juice. Add 2 sliced peaches, 1 sliced and seeded orange, and 1 each cored and sliced Granny Smith and Gala apple. Cover and chill several hours. Stir in 2 cups 7-Up just before serving. Yummm!

The longer you let sangria set, the fruitier it becomes.

Zesty orange
adds a nice zing!

MULLED CHERRY BARS

1 orange

1½ C. flour

1 C. old-fashioned oats

½ C. sugar

¼ C. dark brown sugar

1½ tsp. baking powder

Salt

1 tsp. cinnamon, divided

½ C. butter, cut into pieces & softened

2 tsp. plus ½ C. red wine, divided

⅓ C. honey

½ (12 oz.) pkg. frozen tart red cherries

¼ tsp. ground cloves

2 T. melted butter

To Make

Zest half the orange and toss the zest into a medium bowl. Add the flour, oats, sugar, brown sugar, baking powder, ¾ teaspoon salt, and ½ teaspoon cinnamon; stir. Toss in the butter pieces and 2 teaspoons wine. Work it all together until coarse crumbs form; refrigerate.

Use a vegetable peeler to remove strips of peel from the remainder of the orange and toss the peel into a medium saucepan. Add the honey, cherries, cloves, remaining ½ teaspoon cinnamon, and remaining ½ cup wine. Set over medium heat. When the liquid gets hot, cover the pan, reduce the heat to medium-low, and simmer for 10 minutes, stirring occasionally. Uncover and cook over medium-high heat about 10 minutes longer, until the cherries are soft and the sauce has started to thicken; mash the cherries slightly. Remove from the heat, discard the orange peel, and stir in a pinch of salt. Let cool for 20 minutes.

Preheat the oven to 350°. Grease an 8 x 8" baking pan and line with parchment paper. Pack ⅔ of the chilled crumb mixture into the bottom of the pan and top with the wine filling. Toss the remaining crumbs over the top and drizzle with melted butter.

Bake for 30 minutes or until light golden brown. Cool completely before cutting.

This recipe was tested with Bordeaux, but you could use any full-bodied red.

61

leave the neck unpainted for extra color if you'd like

Say-it-with-wine Chalkboards

Empty wine bottles

Baking soda

Vegetable oil

Paper towels

Chalkboard paint*

Spray paint *(any color)*

Painter's tape

Foam brush

Waxed linen cord

Glue, optional

Chalk

62

* We recommend using chalkboard spray paint for painting entire bottles and brush-on paint for small areas.

To Make

1. Remove the labels from the bottles *(dipping them in warm water will help)*.

   Try this: To remove glue residue, stir together 1 tablespoon each baking soda and oil for each bottle; spread over the residue and walk away for 20 minutes. If the residue doesn't wipe off easily with a paper towel, give it another 10 minutes. It should wipe right off. Rinse bottles and dry well.

2. To paint an entire bottle with chalkboard paint, simply spray on a few coats, letting dry between coats. For bottles with a small chalkboard area, first spray the bottle with a few coats of colored paint, letting dry between coats. Tape off an area for the chalkboard and brush on a few coats of chalkboard paint, letting dry between coats. Carefully remove tape.

3. Begin winding the cord *(it's sticky)* tightly around the bottle, keeping a little of the end exposed. Cover the exposed end with the cord as you continue to wind. Each new row of cord should touch the previous row. When you're ready to stop, just tuck the end up under the previous row or secure it with a dot of glue, if needed.

4. Write a fun message with chalk.

Sharpen the chalk for fine details.

Index